BOSNIA

The Struggle for Peace

Sherry Ricchiardi

THE MILLBROOK PRESS

Brookfield, Connecticut

Published by The Millbrook Press, Inc.
2 Old New Milford Road
Brookfield, CT 06804
© 1996 Blackbirch Graphics, Inc.

5 4 3 2 1

Created and produced in association with Blackbirch Graphics.
Series Editor: Tanya Lee Stone

Library of Congress Cataloging-in-Publication Data

Ricchiardi, Sherry.
    Bosnia: the struggle for peace / Sherry Ricchiardi. — 1st ed.
    p.   cm. — (Headliners)
    Includes bibliographical references and index.
    ISBN 0-7613-0031-7 (lib. bdg.)
    1. Yugoslav War, 1991—Juvenile literature. 2. Bosnia and
Hercegovina—History—1992—Juvenile literature. I. Title. II. Series.
DR1313.5.R53   1996
949.702'4—dc20   95-50478
                                                                      CIP
                                                                      AC

Contents

Chapter 7

Living Under the Gun

A young journalist with sad eyes was describing the details of the most horrifying assignment of his career when, suddenly, his voice trailed off. An eerie silence settled as the flashback from February 5, 1994, took hold of him: bodies strewn on the ground and on the market stalls; the pitiful cries of the maimed pleading for help as they lay bleeding in the snow.

"It was like a meat market," Vlado Staka recalls of the incident that stunned the world: A high-powered shell fired by Bosnian Serb soldiers from the surrounding hills exploded in the outdoor marketplace in Sarajevo, a major city in the former Yugoslavia. The explosion killed 69 and wounded more than 200 citizens.

The struggle for peace persists throughout war-torn Bosnia.

Opposite:
Sarajevo has been the target of violence since the siege that began in April 1992. Here, a marketplace in Sarajevo is shelled in February 1994.

That afternoon, the agony of what happened in Sarajevo hung heavily in the newsroom of the city's largest and most influential daily newspaper. The reporters had the grim task of recording what would become known as "the market massacre." The newspaper's downtown office was located a short distance from where the blast had created mass panic among people already shell-shocked by a year and a half of war in the republic of Bosnia-Herzegovina, or simply Bosnia.

Vlado Staka and his coworkers are among the thousands of Sarajevans who have experienced the torment of living under the constant threat of being killed or wounded. In a split second, a shell might explode on a street or on a playground, or turn an apartment building into a tomb. Snipers wander the bomb-scarred

The reporters for *Oslobodenje* risk their lives to continue to report the news to Sarajevans.

neighborhoods, taking deadly aim at anyone who drifts into their gun sights.

The grisly images that Staka recorded in the newspaper *Oslobodenje*—which means "liberation"—were broadcast to the world via Cable News Network (CNN), the Associated Press (AP), and other media.

As a result of the siege of Sarajevo, which began in April 1992, more than 15,000 people have died in the Bosnian capital. At least 1,500 children have fallen victim to the big guns and sharpshooters. Many more have been wounded.

There was a great international outcry in the aftermath of the violence in February 1994. The North Atlantic Treaty Organization (NATO) demanded the Serbs pull back their heavy weapons to 12.5 miles outside of Sarajevo. This command, however, provided only a brief rest from the violence.

Another Massacre

On August 28, 1995, history repeated itself. This time, the powerful explosion that rocked an outdoor shopping area in Sarajevo, killing 38 and leaving dozens wounded, sparked a quick reaction from the world. NATO sent airplanes streaking into the skies to bomb Serbian positions in retaliation. Many of these NATO missions were flown by American pilots.

Once again, the Serbs—the people primarily held responsible for these actions—were ordered to remove their heavy weapons from around Sarajevo. At first, the Serb leaders refused, but within days, the first signs of Serbian retreat sent rays of hope to war-weary civilians. For the first time in months, humanitarian aid began flowing into the city. By October, the Sarajevan population was again enjoying such basics as running water, food supplies, and electricity.

Soldiers from the UN Rapid Reaction Force surround the area outside Sarajevo to prevent cease-fire violations.

A New Truce Takes Hold

In the wake of the NATO attacks, a new cease-fire was signed by the three main warring groups, the Serbs, Croats, and Muslims—those who embrace the Islamic faith. (Almost half of the Bosnian population is Muslim.)

To guard the fragile cease-fire in fall 1995, a UN Rapid Reaction Force, made up of highly trained combat troops, was sent to patrol the area around Sarajevo. Unfortunately, news reports told of numerous cease-fire violations that threatened the halt of the bloodshed that had tormented the region since 1991, when the former Yugoslavia splintered.

The breakup of the nation of Yugoslavia ignited the bloodiest European conflict since World War II, when the Nazi regime in Germany marched throughout Europe killing millions of people for their religious and ethnic differences. In Croatia and Bosnia, by December 1995, more than 250,000 people had become casualties of the war in the Balkans (a term used to describe the area of Europe that includes the former Yugoslavia, Greece, and Albania).

Frontier Land of Rivalries

What caused this violent outbreak in the former Yugoslavia?

This region has been plagued by religious and cultural turmoil for more than 1,500 years. During the sixth century, the first Slav tribes arrived in the Balkans from the northeast. Many of them were warriors who raided the ancient, but crumbling, Roman Empire.

By this time, Rome had embraced Christianity, but the empire had split in two. The eastern section became known as the Byzantine Empire, and later Constantinople. (Today it is the Turkish city of Istanbul.) As a result of the division in Rome, the Christian church also split into the Orthodox Christian and the Roman Catholic Church. In the Balkans, the dividing line between the two halves of the Roman Empire followed the River Drina, which today marks Serbia's western frontier with Bosnia.

By the seventh and eighth centuries, various groups of Slavs had fallen under the influence of more powerful peoples who invaded from outside Yugoslavia. This domination by foreign forces would affect their future, right up to the present day.

Between the late eighth century and the eleventh century, foreign rule created religious differences among the Serbs, Croats, and Slovenes that today still separate these peoples. The Croatians tend to be Roman Catholics, the

King Alexander ruled the Kingdom of Yugoslavia.

Serbs Christian Orthodox, and many Bosnians of either Serbian or Croatian ancestry are Muslims.

In the late 1300s, the Turks invaded the Balkan region and dominated it for more than 500 years.

The Creation of Yugoslavia

In 1912, Serbia, Bulgaria, Montenegro, and Greece joined forces to drive the last remaining Turks out of the area. During World War I, the Balkan states had shifting alliances to other European countries. Serbia fought the Austro-Hungarians, the Germans, and the Bulgarians. After World War I, in 1918, the boundaries of Europe were redrawn. The prince of Serbia, Alexander, was made head of a new country called the Kingdom of Serbs, Croats, and Slovenes.

In 1929, King Alexander declared his dictatorship over a new country called the Kingdom of Yugoslavia.

World War II

During World War II, Yugoslavs fought against their occupiers—and one another—in the midst of the conflict.

By 1941, Yugoslavia was almost surrounded by German and Italian forces (the Axis). The government signed a treaty with the two Axis powers that many Yugoslavs resented. Two days after it was signed, army officers took over the government.

Less than two weeks later, Axis enemies invaded Yugoslavia. With the Germans and Italians were Hungarians, Bulgarians, and Albanians. The war ended in a couple of weeks, leaving the Yugoslavian government helpless. An armistice was signed with the Axis powers that carved up Yugoslavia into little bits. Germany and Italy shared Slovenia. Italy took Montenegro and the Adriatic coast of Croatia. Albania was given Kosovo. Hungary was given land near its border. Bulgaria occupied Macedonia. And in Belgrade, the capital of Serbia and Yugoslavia, the Germans took over.

On April 10, 1941, while Yugoslavia was being carved up, the government of Croatia proclaimed itself an independent state. It had been sympathetic to the Germans and Italians during the war. For its allegiance, Croatia was given Bosnia. Later, when Italy surrendered, Croatia was also given the Adriatic coast, which it retains to the present day.

With Axis backing, the Croatian government took action against Serbs, Jews, and Gypsies. Those who resisted were killed. The Croatian government assisted the German Nazis in their campaign of extermination against the Jews. The Serbs have not forgotten what happened in World War II. Many of them still have great hatred and very real fear of Croats. (Some Muslims and Serbs also aided the Nazis.)

The Resistance

The Yugoslavs were a determined group of people. Within a few months of the Axis invasion, Yugoslav resistance units formed. One group, the Chetniks, was organized by a Yugoslav army general named Draza Mihailovic. The group's aim was to restore Serbian dominance in Yugoslavia.

Another group, the Partisans, was led by Marshal Tito. Tito sought to organize Yugoslavs of all backgrounds.

The two groups tried to cooperate, but they couldn't. Unfortunately, while both groups were battling the Germans, Italians, and Croats, they also fought each other.

Eventually, Tito's Partisans won the support of the United States, Great Britain, and the other Allies. Tito formed a council to set up a new Yugoslavian government when the war was over. With the aid of the Soviet

Union, the Partisans established a new government with Tito at the head.

Tito executed Mihailovic and stamped out all other opposition. Then he set up the government of Yugoslavia that existed until 1991 as the Socialist Federal Republic of Yugoslavia. It was made up of six republics: Serbia, Croatia, Bosnia-Herzegovina, Slovenia, Macedonia, and Montenegro. Each republic had its own government and also took part in the federal government. It was a Communist state and Tito would not allow different ethnic and religious groups in the country to not tolerate one another. Tito's goal was to create one nation, indivisible, at any cost.

As a Communist state, Yugoslavia had strong ties to the Soviet Union. But Tito had his own ideas about how his country should be run. In 1948, he split with the

Marshal Tito ruled Yugoslavia until his death in 1980.

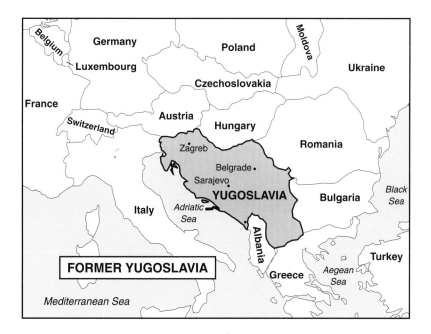

FORMER YUGOSLAVIA

Soviets. Without the Soviet Union as an ally, Yugoslavia was linked neither to the east nor the west. Tito, named president for life, developed a unique Yugoslavian form of communism.

As long as Tito lived, he held the country together by force. He balanced his government carefully between Eastern and Western powers. And he kept Yugoslavia's many rival groups in check. The country became so dependent on its president that, almost as soon as Tito died in 1980, Yugoslavia began to unravel.

The Republics Want Independence

In the post-Tito era, the government "watered down" its communism. Some private enterprise was allowed, and the republics and their ethnic groups were given more power. The more power the republics got, the more they wanted. And republics such as Croatia and Slovenia began to resent the fact that the federal government was dominated by Serbs. Serbia, as it had been many times in the past, was the power in Yugoslavia.

By the middle of the 1980s, anti-Serbian unrest was growing steadily. The federal government cracked down hard on civil protests, but unrest continued. At the same time, the country was beset by serious economic woes.

Inflation reached a staggering 80 percent in 1984. The Socialist system that had been created under the Communists was not working well. Economic problems and unrest caused friction within the Communist party. Under the weight of great criticism and discontent, the Communist party collapsed, and many other parties were declared legal. In the short term, these circumstances may have been good for democracy, but they were not good for the Yugoslavian federation. Movements for greater independence in Slovenia and Croatia grew even stronger. The breakup of Yugoslavia was about to begin.

In 1990, some of the six republics that made up Yugoslavia decided they wanted self-rule. Croatia voted for independence in May 1990 and by June 25, 1991, Croatia and Slovenia declared independence. Bosnia-Herzegovina and Macedonia followed.

All that was left of the Yugoslav federation was Serbia—the largest and most powerful of the republics—and tiny Montenegro. Suddenly, instead of "Yugoslavs," Serbs living in Croatia, for instance, became Croatian Serbs. Croatians living in Bosnia became Bosnian Croats. Loyalties were quickly complicated, as many people of all ethnic backgrounds had made friends and had intermarried. Tensions grew on all sides.

Ethnic Cleansing Tears Region Apart

The perceived need by some for ethnic cleansing in the Balkans has also been an underlying source of violence. "Ethnic cleansing" is a term defined as the ruthless

ETHNIC MAJORITIES OF THE REPUBLICS

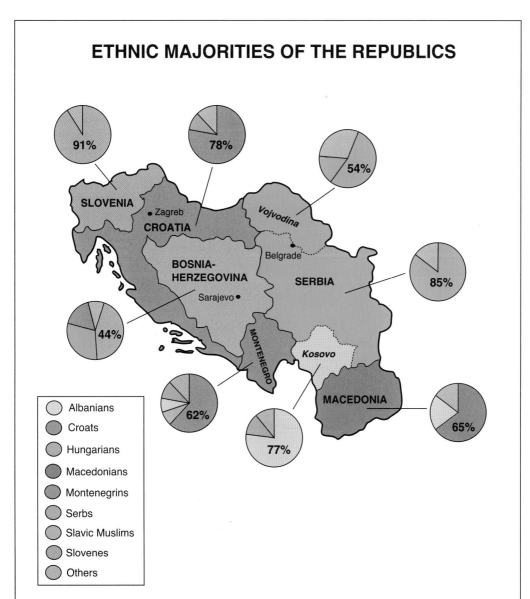

Legend:
- Albanians
- Croats
- Hungarians
- Macedonians
- Montenegrins
- Serbs
- Slavic Muslims
- Slovenes
- Others

Besides the Serbs, Croats, and Slavic Muslims, Yugoslavia has several other peoples. The Montenegrins are closely tied by religion and blood with the Serbs. The Slovenes, centered in Slovenia, are mainly Roman Catholic. Macedonians are largely Orthodox and have strong ethnic ties to both Slavs and Greeks. There are two provinces in Serbia that are largely self-governing. The majority of people in the province of Kosovo are of Albanian blood and Muslim faith. Vojvodina has large numbers of Hungarians and Slovaks, mostly Roman Catholic. Other ethnic groups in Yugoslavia include Italians, Romanians, and Bulgarians. There are many Germans in Croatia.

Memories of My Childhood

Is This a Life?

Is this a kind of life?
There's no sun nor freedom for us.
Is the blue sea really blue?
The Adriatics are now BLACK.
Are the green fields really green?
In Sisak [a Croatian city], the oil fields are burning.
Yes, and this is life as well.
Mother, Father, Sister and myself
loving and longing for peace and freedom.
                                    –Nika, age 10

By December 1995, at least 1,500 of Sarajevo's children had been killed. Most of the children in Bosnia lost at least one member of their family during the 44 months of war.

Psychological scars are likely to haunt these young witnesses to Europe's worst war since the 1940s when Adolf Hitler's army invaded. "The first child I talked with saw his father killed in front of him," says Dr. Arshad Husain, an American psychiatrist who is helping to train mental health workers in Bosnia. The child was 10 years old.

Just like soldiers who return from the battle-field, many of the children of Croatia and Bosnia suffer from post-traumatic stress syndrome, a disorder similar to that experienced by Vietnam veterans. They have flashbacks, nightmares, and suffer from extreme depression.

Art therapy is one way that local teachers, social workers, and other helping agents attempt to draw out the horror these youngsters hold inside. Often, the pictures these children produce are shocking: Some show bodies in graves with their throats slit. There are images of tanks firing on houses; of monsters devouring human beings.

During the years between 1991 and 1995, there was evidence that snipers actually targeted children, particularly in Sarajevo. "They know to kill a child is to strike at the very heart of society. It demoralizes the family and everyone else," said Dr. Barbara Kazanis, an art therapist from Tampa, Florida, who has analyzed dozens of drawings that

attempt by one ethnic group to "purify" the region by driving out all the others. Religious and ethnic differences have long existed in this region.

Tragically, the idea of ethnic cleansing has persisted and is a trademark of the war in the Balkans. Serbian officials have used the term "ethnic cleansing" to describe the mass migrations they have forced from territories that their forces had conquered in Croatia and Bosnia.

People who have been sent to officially monitor human rights violations have documented that the Serbs have driven more than 2 million Muslims and Croats from their homes in Bosnia. Some of these refugees have been tortured and killed, while others have been abused and terrorized by the Serbs.

These drawings are from a collection created by Bosnian and Croatian children who witnessed the war and participated in an art therapy project in Croatia in 1993.

have been created by Bosnian and Croatian children. "Killing a child undermines the very fiber of a country," Kazanis said.

In one survey, researchers found that 900 out of 1,000 children interviewed in Sarajevo said they did not want to live. Many claimed they didn't fear death, but worried constantly about being maimed—losing an arm or leg, or being blinded. Dr. Husain warned that the depression, sleep disorders, and lack of concentration might worsen when and if peace comes. Now, he says, the children spend their energy surviving and staying alive. "When things are calmer, the horror could come back ten-fold," he added.

As the war continued to rage in the Balkans, the Muslims and Croats struck back with some ethnic cleansing of their own. When Serb separatists—those who refused to live under either Croatian or Bosnian rule—conquered a region of Croatia in 1991 that is known as the Krajina, they orchestrated a reign of terror to force Croatians out. In retaliation, when the Croatian army retook this territory in August 1995, a total of 200,000 Serbs packed up and ran for their lives.

The problems in the Balkans are complex. As you have read, the tensions go back over a thousand years. To understand this crisis, it is important to consider both the past history of the region as well as the internal fighting that began in 1991.

Chapter 2

The Balkan Quagmire

The war in the Balkans is often thought to have been ignited by the siege of Sarajevo in the republic of Bosnia-Herzegovina in April 1992. But six months earlier, Serb forces began their brutal attack in the republic of Croatia.

The First Domino to Fall

In Croatia, there is a popular saying: "Before Sarajevo, there was Vukovar." To peacekeepers from the United Nations who were stationed in this region, it was known as Sector East, a small part of Croatian territory that Serb forces controlled after taking the region in November 1991.

To the Croatians, the fallen Vukovar—once a thriving city—carried heavy symbolism. It represented a courageous last stand by an out-gunned, out-numbered

The lack of a unified front against the Serbs quickly complicated the war.

Opposite:
Croatians were moved out of their homes when the Serbs took Vukovar in November 1991.

defense force. The symbol of Serb-occupied Vukovar triggered strong patriotism in Croatia as they refused to surrender to the Serbs.

Reporter Roger Cohen of *The New York Times* wrote: "Before Sarajevo, in 1991, came the Serbian destruction of Vukovar, one of the most ethnically mixed and beautiful towns in Croatia. Today, Vukovar still lies in ruins, its battered water tower looming over the rubble like a gruesome sentry."

Vukovar, located across the Danube River from Serbia, had a pre-war ethnic makeup that reflected the region as a whole. Of the 80,000 pre-war residents of Vukovar and the surrounding area, 44 percent were Croats and 37 percent were ethnic Serbs. The rest were Hungarians, and others.

First Reported Atrocities

When Vukovar fell to the Serbs in November 1991, the Croatians were outgunned by the Yugoslav Army—once the main military force in Yugoslavia. The Croatians fought with mostly light arms and were overpowered by Serbian tanks and heavy artillery.

In the aftermath of the surrender, there were reports of mass killings. The list of missing quickly grew. In January 1993, international investigators sent to the area sealed off mass grave sites that they believed contained bodies of wounded Croatian soldiers who had been dragged out of the Vukovar hospital, taken to a field outside of town, and executed.

In November 1995, four years after the fall of Vukovar, an article in *The New York Times* noted that this was "the first reported atrocity of the Serbian aggression in the former Yugoslavia." Although forensic experts have not yet been allowed to examine the grave sites at Vukovar, any evidence they obtain will be presented to the War Crimes Tribunal in the Netherlands, a panel of judges

that has been appointed to evaluate the evidence gathered against those accused of crimes against humanity during this war.

Some critics have blamed the lack of western intervention during the destruction of Vukovar for the spread of war to other regions of Croatia and to Bosnia-Herzegovina. Warren Zimmerman, America's ambassador to the former Yugoslavia from 1989–1992, commented in the March/April 1995 issue of *Foreign Affairs* magazine that had the international community acted when Croatian cities first were attacked, the Serbian war machine might have been stopped.

The fall of Vukovar was a precursor to the siege of Sarajevo in April 1992.

International War Crimes Tribunal

Following World War II, war crime trials were held in Nuremberg, Germany. Judges at the trials sentenced 12 Nazi leaders to death and imprisoned 7 others. Fifty years later, the International War Crimes Tribunal in the Netherlands began documenting atrocities similar to those committed by Adolf Hitler's army. This time, the accused hailed from the Balkan region of Europe.

By November 1995, 43 Serbs and 6 Croats were charged with committing war crimes and international warrants for their arrests were issued. The charges were serious: Genocide—or wholesale destruction of a group of people, such as the Bosnian Muslims—and other crimes against humanity.

As of December 1995, however, only one person, Dusan Tadic, had been taken into custody for commiting war crimes. The Bosnian Serb was charged with 132 separate counts of crimes against humanity.

A parade of witnesses appeared before television cameras at the Tribunal and told of the crimes supposedly committed by another Bosnian Serb, Dragan Nikolic, the commander of a detention camp called Susica. Nikolic, who in December 1995 remained uncaptured, was charged with the murder, torture, and mutilation of Muslim prisoners.

One witness testified that Nikolic told prisoners that he was "God and the law" inside the camp and that he often terrorized them by putting his gun, which they did not know was unloaded, to their heads or mouths and pulling the trigger.

The war crime trials have been hailed as a breakthrough for international human rights. By December 1995, the War Crimes Tribunal court had reviewed 65,000 pages of documents, 300 hours of videotapes, and other materials. They are determined to continue to identify and punish people who have committed war crimes.

Early Peace Efforts

In 1991, it became clear to the world that the war was quickly escalating and that something needed to be done to achieve peace in the Balkans. Although many people blamed the United States and the European Community (EC) for looking the other way, the U.S. government decided not to become involved with efforts to stop the violence. At the time, the risks seemed to outweigh the benefits.

In June 1991, U.S. Secretary of State James Baker flew to the Serbian capital of Belgrade to explain U.S. policy. Baker told the world that the West supported a united Yugoslavia and urged Slovenia and Croatia to end their bids for independence. Some viewed Baker's statements as a green light for the Yugoslav Army to attack the lightly armed, poorly organized Croatian defense force.

By early 1992, the United Nations decided it was time to get involved and began sending a peacekeeping force to Croatia. The number of peacekeepers sent to the Balkans eventually reached 40,000.

In addition, UN Secretary-general Boutros Boutros-Ghali had appointed Cyrus Vance, a veteran U.S. diplomat, as special UN representative for the former Yugoslavia. Vance was to attempt to negotiate peace in the area. His proposals for a solution became known during negotiations as the Vance Plan. But the final stage, which promised that all displaced persons would be returned to their towns and villages, never came to pass.

The Total Breakup

During April 1992, the brutal pounding of Sarajevo quickly became the symbol of Serbian military aggression in Bosnia-Herzegovina. The American media gravitated toward the city, which had gained fame as host to the 1984 Winter Olympics.

The images that had paraded across television screens in 1984 portrayed an exotic, colorful region—a blend of old-world Eastern with modern Western culture. In the Turkish quarter there were ancient mosques and cozy cafes that served thick black coffee in tiny cups. Artisans along winding cobblestone passageways pounded out beautiful, intricate copper carvings. Some of the designs were centuries old and reflected the Turkish—or Ottoman—influence.

Sarajevans also were accustomed to an urban lifestyle— there were department stores, supermarkets, theaters, and noisy rock clubs. Visitors could sample native dishes at a 15th century warehouse that had been turned into an eatery or dine at the modern Holiday Inn with its flashy floorshows.

The world was proud of the multi-ethnic mix in Sarajevo, a modern European city less than an hour's

Cyrus Vance, representing the United Nations, was involved with early peace-keeping efforts in Bosnia.

flight from Rome, Italy. A walking tour might have begun at the Gazi Husrev Beg mosque that was built in 1531, proceeded to the 16th century Sephardic Synagogue, then to the Christian Orthodox Church (constructed around 1540), and finally to the newer Roman Catholic Cathedral. Sarajevo was a rich city that both preserved old and diverse cultures and accepted the new.

At the time of the 1984 Winter Olympics, the city of Sarajevo and the republic of Bosnia-Herzegovina were part of Yugoslavia. The six republics of Yugoslavia all had their own ethnic flavor.

Following Croatia's and Slovenia's declaration of independence, Bosnia-Herzegovina voted overwhelmingly for independence from Yugoslavia in February 1992. The country's Serbian minority—the Bosnian Serbs—boycotted the election and soon after went on the attack in Bosnia. Serbia wanted to remain the largest and most powerful republic. But both the European Community

THE NEW YUGOSLAVIA IN 1992

and the United States recognized Bosnia's authority to declare independence.

The Bosnian Serbs, as well as the Croatian Serbs, however, were supported by the powerful Yugoslav Army under the direction of Serbian President Slobodan Milosevic. Their aim was to carve out Serbian territories within the new states and link them with Serbia proper. This goal had prompted the attacks against Croatia in 1991. Political analysts believe that the Serbian government under Milosevic plotted to create a "Greater Serbia" that would include parts of Croatia and Bosnia.

Along the River Drina, the historical border between Bosnia and Serbia, and all along the northern part of Bosnia-Herzegovina, heavily armed Serb forces—some of them Bosnian Serbs, some from Serbia proper—crashed their way into unarmed Muslim and Croat villages, carrying out a well-planned campaign of forced expulsion.

Tens of thousands of refugees poured out of Bosnia into neighboring Croatia where they awaited relocation to other countries. Croatia already had become caretaker to hundreds of thousands of its own citizens displaced by the war.

Cultural Heritage Targeted

Almost immediately after the Serbian attacks in Bosnia began, Sarajevo's cultural icons, as well as the Kosevo Hospital overflowing with wounded, became primary targets.

Since April 1992, the Gazi Husrev Beg mosque has sustained more than 150 direct hits from Serbian-fired shells. The National Library, filled with ancient documents, was bombarded and eventually burned down. Sarajevans, under heavy sniper fire, formed a human chain to save a few precious pieces of their history.

Sarajevo's pre-war population was about 250,000. By November 1995, the city held 380,000, swollen by

In Sarajevo during the siege, simply collecting water for daily use was a dangerous task.

refugees who had fled other war-torn areas of Bosnia. Sarajevo had spent 43 terror-filled months under siege. Often, the grisly scenes of ordinary people crumpled in bloody heaps along streets and sidewalks were transmitted via the media to the world.

The day-to-day fear was really what held Sarajevo prisoner. Those who ventured out for food had to traverse Sniper Alley, an area targeted by Serbian sharpshooters. Since fuel was desperately short, walking miles for water, firewood, and other necessities became part of people's harrowing daily routine.

Dateline: Sniper Alley

Since April 1992, the journalists at *Oslobodenje*, Sarajevo's leading daily newspaper, have covered the destruction of their 600-year-old city with its mixed population of Muslims, Croats, and Serbs. The newspaper, and the publishing house that adjoined it, were among the first institutions targeted by Serb forces who seemed determined to drive them out of business.

Through it all, *Oslobodenje* has not missed a single day of publication. Beyond the danger of being hit by a bullet when walking out the door, *Oslobodenje*'s staff has endured working to meet deadlines in its underground quarters—an atomic bomb shelter—as the building shook from bombardments above and was engulfed in flames.

The paper's newsprint, carried across enemy lines, has been confiscated at gunpoint by the Serbs, and delivery drivers have quit in fear for their lives. So, reporters and editors have also sold the newspaper. Perhaps in part because of the staff's perseverance, the newspaper has become a symbol of hope and resistance for the weary city.

In November 1995, after 43 months of war coverage, the toll was heavy: Five of *Oslobodenje*'s employees had been killed, 25 wounded, and 10 correspondents listed as missing in Serb-occupied territory.

Among the dead were a reporter shot at close range while filing a story on the destruction of a Bosnian town, a photojournalist hit by shell-fire while taking pictures of Sarajevans standing in a water line, and a secretary felled by a sniper's bullet as she left the office. "None of our staff was left untouched," says Gordana Knezevic, a deputy editor.

The battle cry for *Oslobodenje*'s staff centered on a single notion: As long as the newspaper was alive, Sarajevo was alive.

It was a war, in fact, that sparked the birth of *Oslobodenje* 52 years ago. The newspaper appeared on August 30, 1943, and became a tool in the underground struggle against the Nazis during World War II. In 1989, *Oslobodenje* was voted paper of the year in Yugoslavia by a nationwide poll of journalists. The daily was one of the first in Bosnia to publish different opinions outside Communist party lines.

In 1984, some of these same journalists were covering a brighter side of life—the glory of the Winter Olympics. Even in 1995, the newsroom of *Oslobodenje* mirrored the ethnic mix of Sarajevo and stood as a beacon against the notion that the three groups no longer can live together.

Situated on the western edge of Sarajevo in one of the city's hottest combat zones, *Oslobodenje* was, at times, no more than 100 meters away from Serb gunners. The street in front is known as "Sniper Alley."

Once, as photographer Senad Gubelic led a visitor through the burned remains of the newspaper building nicknamed 'The Ruins,' he noted, "I call this the disco corridor. Some nights the whole place is lit up by tracer fire [the light that trails gun fire]. It looks like a nightclub, and the noise is deafening...Now you can see the aggressor's positions. They are 50, maybe 100 meters away. I can hear them singing their patriotic songs at night. Sometimes they drive a tank around that playground."

As Gubelic pointed across the way, shots rang out. "We're among their favorites," he joked. "I think they like us a lot."

The photographers and reporters of *Oslobodenje* risk their lives to continue to cover the news in Sarajevo.

The Violence Spreads

Sarajevo was not the only Bosnian target of the Serbs. In Bosnian cities such as Prijedor, Foca, and Sanski Most, the violence against civilians and the destruction of a cultural heritage was also routine.

Mosques in these towns and villages were blown up and plowed under, as if they had never existed. Curfews were established for both Muslims and Croats. Property, such as houses, cars, and tractors, was confiscated. Non-Serbs were demoted from top jobs; some were taken to concentration camps where they lived in horrid conditions.

During testimony before the Commission on Security and Cooperation in Europe (CSCE), Andras J. Riedlmayer, Islamic art and architecture expert from Harvard University, noted: "We are still being told that 'ancient hatreds' are what fuels this destruction, but that is not true. The history that is being erased, both buildings and documents, speaks eloquently of centuries of . . . tolerance in Bosnia. It is evidence of a successfully shared past that the nationalists seek to destroy."

By the end of 1993, almost all of the 200 mosques in the Serb-controlled city of Banja Luka and surrounding areas in Bosnia had been destroyed. At least half of the Roman Catholic churches in the area were also blown up.

In CSCE hearings, testimony indicated that more than half a million Muslims, Croats, Gypsies, Jews, and other non-Serbs had been killed or run out of the Banja Luka region alone.

The Fall of Mostar

As tempers flared and defenses went up, aggression from all sides developed. By 1993, Bosnian Croat extremists began their campaign of ethnic division in the picturesque Bosnian city of Mostar and its mountainous surroundings.

Mourners visit the grave
sites of Bosnian Muslims.

Renaming the region Herceg-Bosna, they set about to rid the area of Muslims. Mate Boban, a native of Bosnia-Herzegovina, was the self-proclaimed leader of this new movement.

Sadly enough, earlier in the war, the Muslims and Croats in Mostar had fought bravely side by side, driving Serbian forces into the hills and saving the town from Serbian occupation.

For Boban and his followers, it was a dark time. They began acting out a destructive scenario similar to that of the Bosnian Serbs. Before it was over, Boban's forces established detention camps for Muslim civilians and set into motion their own vicious brand of ethnic cleansing.

The Muslims and Christians had lived together harmoniously in Mostar for 500 years. Yet, in September 1993, troops under Boban's command began blowing up mosques and rounding up the Muslim population to march them off to camps.

The Bosnian Croats in Mostar also targeted another cultural treasure—the 500-year-old stone Turkish bridge that had for centuries served as a symbol of the city's multi-ethnic tradition. After days of being targeted by fire from the big guns, the bridge crumbled into the river below.

Before it was over, Mostar lay in smoldering ruins, the Muslims living on the east side of the Neretva River, the Croats on the west.

For months, journalists and international aid agencies were denied access to the Mostar area. One British reporter who made his way into the Dretelj detention camp described the brutal scene: "Their [the prisoners'] huge, burning eyes, cropped heads and shrivelled sickly torsos emerged only when one became accustomed to the darkness: hundreds of men, gaunt and horribly thin,

Bosnian Croat extremists targeted Mostar and drove apart Muslims and Croats who had shared the city for hundreds of years.

crammed like factory farm beasts into two stinking underground storage hangars built into the hillside."

In hushed whispers, out of the ear-shot of guards, the prisoners told of being kept in darkness for up to 15 days at a time and existing on one meager meal a day. There were reports of beatings and other torture.

After a series of cease-fires, the ruined city of Mostar came under the administration of the European Union in an attempt to revive the multicultural existence. UN protective forces helped patch differences between people who for centuries had shared a common way of life.

The Six "Safe Havens"

Although all sides have been involved in the brutality, the Serbs have been regarded as the worst aggressors. In a desperate effort to save the Bosnian Muslim and Croat population from Serbian aggression, the United Nations declared six "safe havens" in Bosnia in 1993. These were intended to be war-free zones protected by the United Nations. From the beginning, these isolated areas were plagued by attacks and were not safe at all. At times, ham radio operators and a handful of UN peacekeepers were the only connection to the outside.

The six safe zones were: 1) Sarajevo: The capital of Bosnia-Herzegovina had been under siege by the Serbs since April 1992. The 1993 declaration of Sarajevo as a safe haven had little effect. 2) Gorazde: The largest city in eastern Bosnia, 42 miles east of Sarajevo and laying at a key crossroads. For months, this city was cut off from humanitarian aid and under constant bombardment. 3) Srebrenica: This was the first UN-declared safe haven to fall into Serb hands. After days of a fierce artillery bombardment, Muslim forces surrendered on July 11, 1995, triggering a mass exodus of nearly 25,000. A pattern of murder, rape, and torture followed the fall of

Srebrenica and thousands remain missing. 4) Zepa: The smallest enclave of about 15,000 fell to the Serbs after Srebrenica. Upon first entering the city, Bosnian Serbs agreed to allow the women, elderly, and wounded to be evacuated. Thousands of men remain missing. 5) Tuzla: The population of this northeastern enclave swelled as refugees from Srebrenica sought safety. The towering mountains to the north are under Serb control and Tuzla is within range of their guns. 6) Bihac: For months, this northwestern enclave of 200,000 was surrounded by hostile forces on all fronts. The area was defended by the

Who Are the Key Players in the Balkan Conflict?

1. Bosnia-Herzegovina: Alija Izetbegovic, president; Mohamed Sacirbey, foreign minister.

2. Croatia: Franjo Tudjman, president; Mate Granic, foreign minister.

3. Yugoslavia (federation of Serbia and Montenegro): Slobodan Milosevic, president of Serbia and de-facto leader of what is left of the former Yugoslavia.

4. Bosnian Serbs: Radovan Karadzic, self-styled president of Bosnian Serbs; General Ratko Mladic, Bosnian Serb commander.

The contract group, key countries that wanted to help the former Yugoslavia achieve peace, included representatives of Britain, France, Germany, Russia, and the United States.

| 1. Alija Izetbegovic | 2. Franjo Tudjman | 3. Slobodan Milosevic | 4. Radovan Karadzic |

Bosnian army's tough 5th Corps. In August 1995, the Croatian army helped the 5th Corps to free Bihac.

In the aftermath of the fall of these zones, the international outcry against the Serbs gained momentum in Europe and the United States. Assistant Secretary of State Richard Holbrooke, the chief U.S. negotiator to the former Yugoslavia, credited the fall of Srebrenica and Zepa with pushing western governments to take action against the Bosnian Serbs. In addition, three months before the fall of Srebrenica and Zepa, territorial gains by the Croatian army and the Bosnian government army signaled what many hailed as a major shift of power away from the Serbs.

Just after the Serbs took Srebrenica in a bloody battle, they expelled Bosnians from the safe haven of Zepa in July 1995.

Chapter 3

The Balance of Power Shifts

By May 1995, a frustrated Croatian government decided to take action. In the four years that had passed since the fall of Vukovar, Croatia had built a more powerful and well-organized military—despite a UN-imposed arms embargo (restriction) since 1992. The Croatian army vowed to recapture the one third of Croatia that remained under rebel-Serb control.

For the first time in four years, the Serbs began to lose power.

A Turning Point

On May 1, 1995, the Croatian army stormed across cease-fire lines in western Slavonia, a region of Croatia under Serb control since 1991. UN peacekeepers were held at bay during the two-day blitz while Croatian forces successfully attained their goal of recapturing some of their occupied territory. The recaptured area is about 75 miles east of the Croatian capital of Zagreb.

Opposite:
The tables turned as the Croatian army recaptured some of their territory. Here, two Croatian soldiers raise their flag in the Krajina region.

The main goal of the Croatian army was to reclaim control of a key highway that runs east from Zagreb across the country toward Serbia and to free towns from Serb control.

The quick, decisive victory signaled the beginning of a major shift of power. At the same time, Bosnian government forces were making territorial gains in neighboring Bosnia-Herzegovina. Serbian forces both in Croatia and Bosnia were on the run.

Parts of the rich Slavonian region of Croatia had been lost after the country declared independence from Yugoslavia in 1991, igniting a rebellion of the Serb minority population. The United Nations had brokered a ceasefire, but tensions had remained high. There were constant reports of skirmishes between the two warring factions. The death toll stood at around 10,000 when the United Nations moved into Croatia in early 1992.

After successfully recapturing part of their land, on May 30, 1995, Croatians celebrated the fifth anniversary of their independence.

On the heels of the May 1995 victory, however, UN officials in Zagreb accused Croatian forces of firing at Serbian civilians fleeing across the Sava River into Serb-held Bosnia. But reports by journalists suggested otherwise.

An Associated Press story filed at the time noted: "Hundreds of bedraggled refugees, drenched with heavy rain, converged on the town [Bosanska Ghradiska] carrying their belongings on foot and riding on tractors. They were protected by retreating soldiers. Croatian Serb tanks and other military vehicles occasionally fired to cover the civilians retreat." The AP report added that this suggested the refugees, who included soldiers, were caught in a cross-fire.

The Croatian government did admit to isolated incidents of abuse but denied that they were part of government policy. The Croatian army quickly opened the towns for journalists and human rights monitors who estimated that approximately 5,000 Serbs had fled.

Earlier in the conflict, the Croatian government had attempted to defuse international criticism of their actions against the Serbian minority—about 12 percent of the 4.7 million population—by passing laws guaranteeing political and cultural rights to the Serbs living within Croatia's borders.

Serbs Shell Zagreb in Retaliation

Immediately following the Croatian recapture of 200 square miles in May 1995, Serbs fired rockets equipped with cluster bombs into the bustling city of Zagreb. Six civilians were killed and nearly 200 were wounded.

Rockets slammed into the Croatian National Theater, a children's hospital, and busy main streets. One landed about 100 yards from the U.S. embassy, sending workers scurrying to shelters. The rockets struck rows of parked cars, shattered windows, and left craters in their wake.

One woman was killed as she waited to board a tram in the heart of town.

Infuriated by the attack, the American ambassador to Croatia, Peter Galbraith, told reporters: "This is an outrageous and disproportionate response to the Croatian [military] action, designed solely to kill as many civilians as possible in a major European capital. It was a vile, repugnant act."

A Second Croatian Offensive

On August 4, 1995, following the Serb retaliation, Croatian forces once again went on the move. The Croatian military called it "Operation Storm."

A predawn attack launched in a region of Serb-controlled Croatia known as the Krajina sparked a mass exodus of around 200,000 Croatian Serbs. In the August 13 *Washington Post*, reporter John Pomfret noted: "A visit to this town [Knin, the capital of the self-proclaimed Serb Krajina] answers a lot of questions about how the Croatian army juggernaut [assault] transformed Knin within 30 hours from a Serb rebel stronghold to a place where today Croatian army soldiers lined up behind newly installed phone booths to chat with their girlfriends."

Pomfret also noted that unlike Serb forces, which tend to randomly spray artillery and mortar fire, killing civilians in cross-fire, the Croatian troops appeared to shoot at main targets such as military barracks, a main government building, and the radio communications linked to the Serbian capital of Belgrade.

The two major Croatian offensives, along with gains by Bosnian government and Bosnian Croat forces, created a new balance of power in the Balkans that appeared to be welcomed by the United States and other western countries.

By summer's end, the Serbs had lost all but 5 percent of the territory they held in Croatia and saw their hold

Serbs are expelled from the Croatian region of Krajina in August 1995.

on 70 percent of Bosnia steadily decrease. It appeared that the dream of a "Greater Serbia" had finally been dealt a lethal blow.

Aftermath of "Operation Storm"

As with the May 1995 offensive, charges of Croatian military abuse in the recaptured Krajina region resurfaced soon after the dust settled on "Operation Storm."

This time the Croatian government began investigating the charges and arrested nearly 375 soldiers and policemen. In one report, nine elderly Serbs were found to have been shot; another report listed 27.

Two of the Most Wanted

Two men seem to be the most responsible for war crimes in the Balkans. They are Radovan Karadzic, the Bosnian Serb leader who once threatened that the Balkan conflict could spark World War III, and Ratko Mladic, the Bosnian Serb general, whose armies have been accused of some of the worst atrocities since the Nazi era in Europe 50 years ago.

Following are sketches of the two men who have been indicted as war criminals by the War Crimes Tribunal. Both stand to be arrested if they leave Serb-held territory.

Radovan Karadzic

The president of the self-proclaimed Bosnian Serb Republic was born in the hills of neighboring Montenegro. Radovan Karadzic's family moved to Sarajevo when he was 15, where he lived for 30 years before emerging as a rebel leader.

Former neighbors remember him as a thin, shy youth, who marched at the head of student demonstrations and waved posters of Tito, the influential leader of the Communist Yugoslav country who died in 1980.

Bosnian Serb commander Ratko Mladic

Though from a poor family, he attended college and medical school, and went on to work as a psychiatrist at Kosevo Hospital in Sarajevo—the medical facility that Bosnian Serb gunmen have targeted, killing and wounding patients.

While in Sarajevo, Karadzic lived in a mixed neighborhood with Roman Catholics, Muslims, and Jews. Yet today, the Bosnian Serb leader argues for ethnic purity, claiming that the various groups no longer can co-exist. From the beginning, Radovan Karadzic was chief among the scheming parties committed to creating Greater Serbia.

Ratko Mladic

Bosnian Serb commander Ratko Mladic graduated from a Yugoslav military academy and joined the Communist party in 1965. Three decades later, the stocky general stands accused of genocide—wholesale destruction of a people—by the International War Crimes Tribunal.

The "bully of the Balkans," as he has been labeled in many news reports, oversaw the shelling of Sarajevo with the most powerful and destructive guns. He also organized the pounding of two UN designated "safe havens," Srebrenica and Zepa, which eventually fell to the Serbs.

When the first "safe haven" of Srebrenica surrendered, Mladic was shown on Serbian television offering chocolate to Muslim children and patting them on the head. Off camera, his soldiers terrorized, raped, and murdered the people of Srebrenica. Thousands of Bosnian Muslims from this area remain missing.

Mladic grew up in a Bosnian village 25 miles south of Sarajevo. There was a hint of what was to come in his name: Rat means "war" in the Serbo-Croatian language, which was spoken throughout the former Yugoslavia.

The commander was quoted in a Bosnian Serb newspaper as saying: "There will be no peace in the Balkans until all Serbs join forces and live in a single country. Serbs should never give up their goal, even if it means another world war."

Croatian President Franjo Tudjman condemned all acts of revenge on Serbs but said many Croatians found revenge hard to resist after being controlled by the Serbs for so long.

The United Nations launched investigations into the alleged abuses in the Krajina. The United Nations, however, as well as other international agencies continued to recognize the Krajina as part of Croatia proper.

In an October 1995 press conference, Croatian President Franjo Tudjman was asked about the charges of human rights abuses in the Krajina. Tudjman noted that 120,000 Croatian refugees had returned to their homes in the Krajina and that some of them could not curb their urge for revenge after four years of being homeless. He condemned all acts of revenge and looting.

Asked by reporters if it was true that Croatia "would not tolerate" the return of Krajina Serbs, Tudjman replied that Serbs who met requirement for Croatian citizenship could return on an individual basis but a "total return" of the 200,000 Serbs could not take place.

Chapter 4

International Intervention

On the heels of battlefield victories, the Croatian army and Bosnian government forces received another boost in attempts to regain territory from rebel Serbs. Sparked by continual attacks against civilians, U.S.-led NATO warplanes began attacking Serb positions.

Operation Deliberate Force was NATO's largest combat mission in the alliance's 47-year history. Serb targets included ammunition dumps, command sites, key bridges, supply routes, and air defense systems.

By mid-September 1995, more than 3,400 missions had been flown—many by American pilots.

Benefiting from the internal turmoil among Serbian forces during the fierce NATO attacks, Croatian and

Once the balance of power shifted, outside intervention increased.

Opposite:
NATO troops were deployed to the Balkans as international concern grew.

Bosnian soldiers recaptured a string of strategic towns, including Jajce, the location of an important power plant and the spot where the Communist state of Yugoslavia was founded by Tito in 1943.

As the NATO bombings continued, Russia (which has historically supported the Serbs) stiffened its efforts to halt NATO. The Russians, however, had no effect. Even so, for a while, even under fierce attack, Bosnian Serb commander Ratko Mladic stubbornly refused to withdraw their guns and tanks.

NATO continued the heaviest pounding the Serbs had taken in four years. Only after Mladic finally began to withdraw did NATO halt the attacks. At the same time, a new U.S.-led plan for peace, spearheaded by American diplomat Richard Holbrooke, was gathering momentum, despite the fact that disaster had struck.

Peacemakers Killed

On August 19, 1995, a U.S. diplomatic team set out in a convoy along a dangerous mountain road into Sarajevo. The group was headed for talks with the Bosnian president. It was, it seemed, an excellent window of opportunity in light of the recent power shifts.

But the group suffered a tragic setback.

Three key members of the peacemaking team were killed when the French armored vehicle in which they were riding plunged off the slippery mountain road into a deep ravine near Sarajevo. Robert Frasure, 53, who was credited with being the chief architect of the new peace plan; Joseph Kruzel, 50, the Pentagon's deputy assistant secretary of defense for European and NATO Policy; and Air Force Colonel Samuel Nelson Drew, 47, a soldier-diplomat attached to the White House National Security Council all lost their lives. One French soldier was also killed in the crash and two other passengers were badly injured.

At the memorial for the deceased, U.S. Defense Secretary William Perry told mourners, "They stood for peace, they died for peace. What they stood for and died for will be strived after for as long as it takes." Almost immediately, a new group was appointed to carry on the work, but it was to be a slow process.

Failure to Act

After more than three years of bloodshed, the Bosnians' faith in the peace process had steadily weakened. There were charges that NATO and the United Nations had set a precedent of not following tough words with strong actions. It often appeared that the two international bodies were at odds about how to combat Serbian aggression.

Even though the UN Security Council, a powerful decision-making body within the United Nations, had authorized the use of force in response to Serbian attacks against the six "safe havens," UN commanders on the ground hesitated to call for NATO air strikes because they feared retaliation against their lightly armed peacekeepers. Indeed, from May 26 to June 18, 1995, Serbs, defying NATO and UN threats, took hundreds of UN soldiers hostage. They did so in an act of revenge for the NATO bombing of ammunition dumps in the Bosnian Serb stronghold of Pale.

The hostages were released only after top UN officials pledged to end the air strikes.

Mass Graves Discovered

In September 1995, investigators in Croatia and Bosnia uncovered new evidence of Serb brutality—mass grave sites. Overwhelmed by the task of examining the vast

UN hostages are welcomed after being released by Bosnian Serbs.

expanse of the killing fields, investigators asked the United States for help.

One expert who answered the call was Dr. Henry Lee, who testified for the defense in the high profile O.J. Simpson trial in the United States. Lee is an expert in examining bodies to determine the circumstances and time of death.

USA Today carried a story in October 1995, that told readers that some of the top scientists from the United States had been plowing the earth of small towns throughout Bosnia and Croatia, examining 25 mass grave sites believed to contain as many as 700 bodies. What they found documented a chilling record of ethnic cleansing.

Henry Lee noted in an interview, "These are the largest and worst mass graves I have seen."

The Evidence Builds

During 1995, as President Milosevic of Serbia was attempting to create a reputation as a peacemaker, *The New York Time*s and other major media presented information to the contrary. In one case, a senior member of the Serbian secret police, Cedomir Mihailovic, provided documents that indicated Milosevic was directly tied to violent events in Bosnia.

Among the documents provided was one dated May 24, 1992, which appears to include directions from the Serbian state security services in Belgrade on the running of concentration camps in Bosnia. *The New York Time*s article noted that President Milosevic was in daily contact with security services.

When the International War Crimes Tribunal for the former Yugoslavia went into session in the Netherlands, lawyers had presented a chilling account of the horrors commited during this war, most of it related by refugees and other eyewitnesses.

The president of Serbia, Slobodan Milosevic, has been linked to the violence that has occurred in Bosnia during this war.

Sword Rattling in Croatia

As negotiations proceeded on ways to end the war in Bosnia, Croatian President Franjo Tudjman, a leader of the country's independence movement, threatened to order military action to reclaim the 5 percent of Croatian land still in Serb hands.

More than 90,000 Croatians expelled from an eastern region of Croatia in 1991 were waiting to go home. And Vukovar, the fallen city that had become the symbol of Croatian resistance, was located in this agriculturally rich region called Eastern Slavonia. Croatians would never be satisfied until Vukovar was back in their hands.

As part of the peace negotiations, the Croatians offered to temporarily keep this eastern section under UN control, but there were conditions attached. The Croatians wanted several things. Serbia would have to recognize

The Daring Rescue of Captain O'Grady

On June 8, 1995, Americans were introduced to a humble new hero. Before sunrise that day, 29-year-old U.S. Air Force Captain Scott O'Grady was rescued after surviving for six nights in hostile Serbian territory, living on ants and grass, hiding by day and moving about at night. O'Grady's F-16 jet was shot down by a Bosnian Serb missile during a NATO patrol of Bosnian skies.

The pilot drew on his strong faith and highly specialized training to avoid capture. He later told the world: "I am no Rambo...I was a scared little bunny rabbit."

O'Grady described how his cockpit fell apart after taking the hit. He remembered looking down to see "the beautiful gold handle of my ejector seat" between his legs. The pilot yanked the handle and parachuted to earth, praying that he wouldn't be spotted by Serbian sharpshooters.

He tore off the parachute and ran for the thick pine forest, his heart pounding as he sought to avoid capture. He dropped into a bushy area and rubbed his face with dirt.

Captain Scott O'Grady arrives in the United States after his rescue.

By that time, Serb patrols were moving through the area, sometimes only a few feet away from O'Grady's hiding place. They fired weapons into the weeds, attempting to flush the American out. Then, on the sixth day behind enemy lines, the break came.

O'Grady had taken cover in a rocky pasture on a clear, starlit night. Suddenly, he heard three faint clicks on his radio. Although barely audible, he made out the words, "Basher 52. This is Basher 11 on Alpha." Basher 52 was O'Grady's call number. Someone was up in the sky searching for him. "Basher 52 reads you loud and clear!" said O'Grady in a hushed tone.

Plans for the daring dawn rescue went into effect. The crews of the Cobra gunships counted on the element of surprise and the soupy fog for cover. They hovered dangerously overhead, a target for Serb gunners, as they searched for a sign of the downed pilot.

O'Grady heard the roar of the Cobras and shot off a flare, sending smoke billowing skyward. He hovered at the edge of the forest waiting for the Marines to land.

In a flash, there he was, dirty, unshaven, and soaking wet, waving a pistol as he ran. The rescuers pulled O'Grady on board and wrapped him in a blanket. The shivering, exhausted pilot managed to mouth the words, "Thank you" to the men who had risked their lives to save him. The story of O'Grady's rescue captured America's heart.

One article noted that in June 1995, O'Grady was mentioned by major media outlets more than 1,500 times. The *Chicago Tribune* dubbed him the "Hero Pilot." *Newsweek* magazine put O'Grady on the cover under the headline "An American Hero." *Newsweek* told readers that the Air Force captain was a member of the Right Stuff Brotherhood whose code was understated: "Cool."

During a speech in the White House rose garden, O'Grady thanked God for sparing his life and designated the Marines who rescued him the real heroes.

President Clinton discusses ways for the United States and the United Nations to help bring peace to the Balkans.

Croatia as an independent state; the Serb military in the area would have to be disarmed; and a local police force would have to be put in place reflecting the ethnic make-up of the area before the war—65 percent Croatians and Hungarians and 35 percent Serbs.

Croatia included these conditions in its overall peace demands. In the meantime, the Yugoslav Army, under the control of Serbian President Milosevic, moved tanks and heavy weapons to within striking distance of the contested region sparking fears of a wider war should Croatia attack.

Still, the United States and other western countries strove to find ways to help end the war. President Clinton talked hopefully of new attempts to bring the warring factions closer to peace in the Balkans.

BOSNIA  PEACE TALKS

Let There Be PEACE On EARTH
And Let IT BEGIN HERE !

FAIRBORN, OHIO

Chapter 5

Peace on the Horizon?

By fall 1995, American involvement in the Balkan conflict was at its peak. Many felt that this was a critical turning point. The Europeans had made little progress—and, some critics charge, too little effort—in stopping the violence. Now, the Clinton administration and key U.S. politicians had taken the lead. Besides the work at the negotiating table, the United States also flexed its military muscle.

By September 1995, two U.S. aircraft carriers, the *USS Roosevelt* and *USS America* were anchored in the Adriatic Sea to help blast Serbian air defenses that threatened NATO pilots. The warships were equipped with Tomahawk cruise missiles that were fired at Serb targets to avoid detection by flying below radar. Because they were fired from ships offshore, they didn't risk the lives of American pilots.

After years of brutal fighting, peace seemed to be attainable.

On November 1, 1995, Bosnian peace talks began in Dayton, Ohio.

The aircraft carrier *USS Roosevelt* was anchored in the Adriatic Sea to help blast Serbian air defenses.

Russians Complain

This stronger U.S. presence and continued NATO threat sparked loud protests from the Serbs' allies—the Russians. Both the Serbs and Russians practice the Orthodox Christian faith and have other common cultural ties. Russia's representative, Vitaly Churkin, accused the United States and NATO of forcing an upsurge in the violence by taking the Bosnian government's side.

Referring to the U.S.-led NATO air strikes, Churkin complained at a press conference, "Such actions only aggravate the crisis and are absolutely impermissible." The Russian government demanded special negotiations to determine what role it would play in helping to police Bosnia if a peace deal was struck. In the end, NATO and Russia reached an agreement and Russia planned to send a contingent to work alongside NATO forces in Bosnia.

Boost for Bosnian Military

The Clinton administration had decided that a balance of military power in the Balkans was necessary if NATO troops were to go into Bosnia to help regulate a peace plan. Officials began to scramble to come up with a plan to help build up the Bosnian government's army to match the fire power of the Serbs in the region.

President Clinton, under fire from Congress for his previous lack of action in the Bosnian war, wanted to assure his critics and the American people that if NATO troops, including Americans, went into Bosnia on the ground, they could be pulled out within a year or two. That would only be possible if the Bosnian government's army had its military strength boosted in order to be a match against the heavily armed Serbs.

U.S. Secretary of State Warren Christopher, Defense Secretary William Perry, and General John Shalikashvili, America's top military officer, appeared before a Senate Armed Services and Foreign Relations panel to answer questions about the proposed role of the United States in the Balkans.

Senators posed several questions. How long would the NATO peacekeeping mission be and how much would it cost? If the United States withdrew its forces after a year, would a NATO or UN force remain? What, exactly, would the NATO mission consist of?

U.S. Secretary of Defense William Perry addressed a panel of senators to answer policy questions regarding the peacekeeping mission in Bosnia.

Key Issues and Risks

Key among many issues raised by Congress was the unanswerable question of how great the risk of casualties would be for American soldiers. Senator James Inhofe, a Republican from Oklahoma, summed up a main point at the heart of the debate: "I'd like to have any one of you tell me, if we're going to have hundreds of young Americans dying over there, is the mission. . .justification for their deaths?"

Early plans called for 60,000 NATO soldiers, including 20,000 from the United States, to be stationed in Bosnia. But, in December 1995, several important questions remained unanswered.

Who would train the Bosnian military? Where would the weapons come from? Who would pay for the equipment and the training? What supplies do the Bosnian army, hampered since the beginning of the war by an arms restriction, really need? And, who ultimately would control the flow of guns, tanks, and other materials into the country?

There was one more snag: U.S. Secretary of State Warren Christopher noted that NATO balked at sending peacekeeping troops to Bosnia as long as two Serb leaders indicted as war criminals held power. Christopher was referring to Bosnian Serb President Radovan Karadzic and General Ratko Mladic.

Beacon of Hope

In response to the bold actions of NATO and the United States, the three presidents—Tudjman of Croatia, Izetbegovic of Bosnia-Herzegovina, and Milosevic of Serbia (the Serbian president was acting on behalf of the Bosnian Serbs)—flew across the Atlantic Ocean to negotiate on American soil. Self-styled Bosnian Serb leader Radovan Karadzic was not in attendance and wrote a letter to western leaders, noting, "It is clear that the most powerful military alliance in the world is openly taking the side of our enemies. The entire peace process can be wrecked."

On November 1, 1995, the warring parties gathered at Wright-Patterson Airforce base in Dayton, Ohio, to talk of peace. At this important crossroads in the conflict, America had become the beacon of hope in the Balkans. American leadership was crucial if the bloodshed was to be stopped.

U.S. Secretary of State Warren Christopher speaks at the peace talks in Ohio. The two men with their backs to the camera are: (left) Milosevic and (right) Tudjman.

President Clinton vowed he would not send American troops into Bosnia as part of the NATO peacekeeping force unless a stable political and military settlement had been signed by all sides.

The biggest turning point in the four-year conflict was the initialing of an agreement at the Ohio peace talks. The agreement was scheduled to be formally signed on December 14, 1995, in Paris.

Unlike previous peace agreements that had failed, this one was driven by widespread exhaustion with this war that has killed thousands, uprooted more than 2 million people from their homes, and shocked the world with terrible human rights violations.

U.S. Secretary of State Warren Christopher, who spent many continuous days and nights hammering out the final details of the agreement, called it "a victory for all those who believe in a multi-ethnic democracy in Bosnia." The secretary added, "It offers tangible hope that there will be no more days of dodging bullets, no more winters of freshly dug graves, no more years of isolation from the outside world."

Not all the parties, however, welcomed the pact.

Bosnian Serbs Balk at Peace

The Bosnian Serbs complained loudly that the 60,000 NATO peacekeepers would really become an occupying force. Indeed, under the Ohio agreement, NATO was given sweeping powers, including the right to relocate troops or weapons at will. This displeased the Serbs who wanted to keep strict control over certain areas of Bosnia.

The Bosnian Serbs were even more upset over the Ohio agreement regarding Sarajevo, which placed many Serb-held neighborhoods under Bosnian government rule. Their leaders charged that Serb civilians would be at risk from Bosnian Muslims and Croats who might seek revenge.

Most important, the peace agreement provided for Bosnia to remain a single state, with its pre-war borders intact. But, it also divided Bosnia into two near-equal parts—one side controlled by a Muslim-Croat federation; the other by a Serb republic. In simple terms, the Bosnian government would give up the 49 percent of its territory under Bosnian Serb control. The plan also included the formation of a central government with a democratically elected president and parliament, the return of all refugees to their homes, and reconstruction of the country.

One key question, however, remained unanswered: How can a government that is made up of enemies who only recently put their weapons down survive in any kind of harmony?

A Success for the United States

In the end, the Ohio peace agreement was a personal success for Warren Christopher and Richard Holbrooke. They, along with a team of veteran mediators, engineered a complicated process in which American influence brought together the three Balkan presidents and chief negotiators from Britain, France, Germany, and Russia.

America's international leadership was in the spotlight. The American strategy for peace in the Balkans hinged on three major points: First, strengthening the Muslim-Croat federation to present a united front against the Serbs. Second, settling the one major territorial dispute left between Serbs and Croats—the return of Vukovar and the territory surrounding it. And third, persuading all three parties that this was the last best chance to end the ruthless pattern of Serb aggression.

U.S. Troops Land in Tuzla

Tuzla, with powerful Serbian guns still dug into the mountains surrounding the town, was designated as the major base for the 20,000 Americans headed to Bosnia and Croatia as part of the NATO peacekeeping forces called "Operation Joint Endeavor." Americans would make up one third of the 60,000-person contingency.

The Americans entered Bosnia with strong fire power and the right to shoot back if challenged, unlike the UN peacekeepers who had served as monitors. President Clinton built support from Americans for the mission.

In November, the president made a televised speech to urge the American people to help the nations of Europe end the violence. President Clinton sent the opinion polls soaring in his favor with the doctrine of leadership he delivered. He told the American people: "We cannot stop war for all time, but we can stop some wars. We can't do everything, but we must do what we can."

Chronology

1984 Economic problems and unrest cause the collapse of Yugoslavia's Communist party.
Independence movements grow in Croatia and Slovenia.

June 1991 Slovenia and Croatia declare independence. Macedonia and Bosnia follow. Federal and Slovenian troops clash on Slovenian borders.

Fall 1991 Extremist Serbs begin their campaign of "ethnic cleansing."
Croats are forced out of eastern Croatia, which becomes Serb-occupied.
A cease-fire is negotiated by the United Nations and accepted in eastern Croatia.

February 1992 UN peacekeepers move into Croatia to ensure the terms of the truce.
Bosnian Croats and Muslims vote for independence.

April 1992 Sarajevo is surrounded, and the siege begins.

July 1992 The United Nations begins airlifts of food and aid to Sarajevo.
Milan Panic becomes prime minister of Yugoslavia but is unable to make constructive changes.

November 1992 The United Nations enforces previous trade sanctions and imposes a naval blockade on Yugoslavia.

January 1993 Croatian army surges past UN cease-fire zones into territory held by rebel Serbs, capturing the bridge and airport near the key coastal city of Zadar.

April 1993 Croat-Muslim fighting erupts in central and southwest Bosnia over the 30 percent of territory not held by the Serbs.

April/May 1993 UN creates six "safe havens" for protection of Bosnian Muslims and Croats.

February 1994 Powerful shell explodes in a Sarajevo marketplace, killing 69 and wounding 200, all civilians.

March 1994 Bosnia's Muslim-led government and Bosnian Croats sign U.S.-brokered peace agreement, ending a bitter year of fighting. U.S. pushes the two sides to create a federation.

November 1994 Serbs detain 55 Canadian peacekeepers as insurance against further NATO air strikes.

January 1995 Four month cease-fire takes hold in Bosnia. The safe haven of Bihac remains under attack.

May 1995 More than 400 peacekeepers are detained.

May 1, 1995 Croatian army launches drive to recapture 200 square miles of occupied territory. Serbs retaliate by firing rockets into Croatian capital of Zagreb.
NATO attacks Serb ammunition dumps for failure to remove heavy weapons around Sarajevo. Serbs retaliate by shelling civilians in "safe haven" of

Tuzla. Seventy-one are killed.

Serbs take up to 370 UN peacekeepers hostage, chaining some to bridges, barracks, and other strategic points to ward off NATO attacks.

June 1995 Serbs shoot down U.S. F-16 over northern Bosnia.

July 1995 Serbs over-run "safe havens" of Srebrenica and Zepa.

August 1995 Croatian army attacks rebel Serb-occupied region of Krajina, sparking mass exodus of around 200,000 Serbs into Serb-held Bosnia and Serbia.

On August 28, two shells hit outdoor market in Sarajevo, killing 38. UN investigators blame Bosnian Serbs. NATO warplanes attack Serb targets in Bosnia in retaliation.

September 1995 NATO air attacks are suspended after more than 750 missions and Serbs pull guns back from around Sarajevo.

November 1, 1995 Delegations led by presidents of Bosnia-Herzegovina, Croatia, and Serbia, arrive in U.S. for peace talks at Wright-Patterson Air Force Base in Ohio.

November 1995 Warring factions initial peace agreement to be officially signed in December.

December 1995 NATO begins to send 60,000 troops, including 20,000 Americans, to Bosnia.

Formal signing of peace treaty takes place in Paris.

For Further Reading

Flint, David. *Bosnia: Can There Ever Be Peace?* Chatham, NJ: Raintree Steck-Vaughn, 1995.

Greene, Carol. *Yugoslavia*. Chicago: Children's Press, 1990.

Ifkovic, Edward. *The Yugoslavs in America*. Minneapolis, MN: Lerner, 1990.

Ricciuti, Edward R. *War in Yugoslavia: The Breakup of a Nation*. Brookfield, CT: The Millbrook Press, 1993.

Rosen, J.A., editor; et. al. *Bosnia Teenage Refugees*. Leverett, MA: Rector Press Limited, 1995.

Index

Acknowledgments and photo credits

Cover and pages 30, 36, 46: ©Krpan Jasmin/Gamma Liaison; p. 4: ©Masao Endo/SABA; p. 6: ©Andrew Reid/Gamma Liaison; pp. 8, 40: ©Laurent Van der Stockt/Gamma Liaison; pp. 10, 12, 48: AP/Wide World Photos, Inc.; p. 17: Children of Croatia/Bosnia Art Project; p. 18: ©Peternek/Eastlight/SABA; p. 21: ©Zeljko/Gamma Liaison; p. 23: ©R. Haviv/SABA; p. 26: ©Peterson/Gamma Liaison; pp. 27, 42: ©Noel Quidu/Gamma Liaison; p. 29: ©Mike Persson/Gamma Liaison; p. 32 (from left to right): ©Haviv/SABA; ©Filip Horvat/SABA; ©Badzic/Eastlight/SABA; ©Haviv/SABA; p. 33: ©Art Zamur/Gamma Liaison; p. 34: ©Gamma Liaison; p. 39: ©Pava/Zamur/Gamma Liaison; p. 41: ©Martin Simon/SABA; p. 47: ©Alain Morvan/Gamma Liaison; p. 49: ©Diana Walker/Gamma Liaison; p. 50: ©Dan Cleary/Gamma Liaison; p. 52: ©Paoni/Contrasto/SABA; p. 54: ©M. Gronemberger/Reporters/SABA; p. 56: ©Ralf-Finn Hestoft/SABA.

Maps and graphics by Blackbirch Graphics, Inc.